Rabbits

JoAnn Early Macken

Reading consultant: Susan Nations

W

FRANKLIN WATTS

LONDON•SYDNEY

First UK hardback edition 2004
First UK paperback edition 2005

Franklin Watts
96 Leonard Street
London EC2A 4XD

Franklin Watts Australia
45-51 Huntley Street
Alexandria
NSW 2015

ISBN 0 7496 5763 4 (hardback)
ISBN 0 7496 5830 4 (paperback)

Published in association with Weekly Reader Early Learning Library, Milwaukee.

Printed in Hong Kong, China

Contents

Baby rabbits

Newborn rabbits have no fur. They cannot see, hear or hop. After two months, they are old enough to be pets.

Short or long fur?

Rabbits may have short fur or long fur. Rabbits with long fur need to be brushed more often.

Colours and patterns

A rabbit's fur may be brown, black, white or a mixture of colours. Your rabbit may have spots or patterns in its fur.

Droopy ears

Rabbits are able to move their ears so they can hear better. Some rabbits have ears that droop. These rabbits are called "lops".

Using its whiskers

A rabbit uses its **whiskers** to find its way in the dark. It can fit into a space that is as wide as its whiskers.

whiskers

Eating and drinking

Rabbits eat food in pellets. They also need fresh water and hay. They like carrots, parsley and other vegetables.

Your rabbit hutch

A rabbit can live in a cage or a hutch. In good weather it can go outside.

Feeling scared

When a rabbit is scared it will thump its feet. It sits up to see or smell things.

Playing

Rabbits can roll balls. They can hop in and out of things. Give your rabbit a toy and watch it play!

New words

hay — dried grass or other plants fed to animals

hutch — a pen or cage for an animal

pellets — small pieces of food

thump — to bang or knock

How to find out more

Here are some useful websites about rabbits:

www.petplanet.co.uk/petplanet/kids/kidsrabbit.htm
How to choose the right rabbit, a shopping list for your rabbit, making friends, training and what your rabbit's noises and actions mean

www.pdsa.org.uk
Click on "You and your pet" and then on "Rabbits". Useful information about looking after your rabbit and some questions and answers.

www.abc.net.au/creaturefeatures/facts/rabbits.htm
An Australian website with pet facts on rabbits and a link to the Australian Companion Rabbit Society website

Note We strongly advise that Internet access is supervised by a responsible adult.

Index

Notes for teachers and parents

This book is specially designed to support the young reader in the reading process. The familiar topic is appealing to young children and invites them to read — and re-read — the book again and again. The full-colour photographs and enhanced text help the child during the reading process. After children develop fluency with the text and content, the book can be read independently.